WATER TABLES

Water Tables

by JAMES SEAY

WESLEYAN UNIVERSITY PRESS

Middletown, Connecticut

The author wishes to thank the Research Councils of the University of Alabama and of Vanderbilt University for grants, which were of great help during the time when he was working on this book.

Acknowledgement is gratefully made to *American Review, The Carolina Quarterly, Southern Poetry Review* and *The Vanderbilt Poetry Review,* in the pages of which some of the poems in this book were first published.

The publisher gratefully acknowledges the support of the Andrew W. Mellon Foundation toward the publication of this book.

Library of Congress Cataloging in Publication Data

Seay, James.
  Water tables.

  (The Wesleyan poetry program, v. 72)
  Poems.
  I. Title.
PS3569.E24W3   811'.5'4   73–15014
ISBN 0–8195–2072–1
ISBN 0–8195–1072–6 (pbk.)

Manufactured in the United States of America
First printing, 1974

92 91 90 89   5 4 3 2

WESLEYAN POETRY

For Josh and Page

Contents

v

I

For Joshua, at His Great-Grandfather's Grave

Unimpressed by all that marks his passing—
words and a name
on the travertine wall, the days and years—
you turn your small face away
to where the trees breathe
a light song,
life from the mountains.

Somewhere in all this green or beyond
can the earth's skin be dying?

I watch stonemasons
lifting the same white marble
to face a near wall of empty vaults.
The foreman shows me blueprints
drawn at the Italian quarry.
One legend translates 'all is marked.'

Will the stream be clear
you put your knee beside?

The stone, of course—
marked in numbers we all can read.
And to that I add your forehead and mine,
your mother's here beside us,
her grandfather's marked in this marked stone,
it is all marked
and I accept
for us all.

I accept
that all is marked for this wall, this valley,

that this is what the numbers add up to,
I accept, I accept,
all but what has been marked against
your green assembly.

The smoke of what we have dug
from these mountains
hangs over every city
like a final trumpet.

Thieves strip off the blanket of topsoil
for the rich darkness that sleeps there.
They leave the slopes without cover
and when it rains, nothing holds.
Miners with black lung
drop into the shafts each morning,
knowing no other way.

Can you hear me?
I am trying to make it right
for when I am words and a name
on the wall, my days
and years all marked.

I am shouting over the walls for you
the message I have found in your looking away:
there is only one faith
and it is written in these leaves.

Naming the Moon

The moon is in the patch of trees on our hill
and so we go out to name and claim it
for the first time together.
No matter that in the window by your bed alone
it has been *airplane* or *car* or *light;*
tonight it is clearly *moon,*
as big and pale as your mother's belly twenty months ago,
though diminishing as it clears our hill
and pulls toward the Milky Way.   *Moon   Moon*
Your small butt stirs against my chest
and as the word takes hold of you like a possession
I sense tides beginning to draw again over fossil shells
in the limestone wall beneath your boots.
A mist like salt spray finds the light hairs
around my nostrils. I know these stars
were where the seas fell. Sand is running out
from under us.
Trying to hold you from the undertow,
yet steadily giving you to the moon,
I almost call out *airplane airplane car light.*
But then I hear your new word turn to *cold*
and realize it is November, not dead waters,
stirring us. We go inside,
you to your bath, I to a whirlpool of words
that become the whirlpool of draining water
you put your finger in to claim whatever is there.
And whatever it is
now as you come naked into my room bringing back to me
trees hill an airplane cowboy boots limestone dead seas a light
I remember it is out of my hands,
for finally, turning, you give me the moon
before I forget.

On the Way

This is the children's road.
No way to find it but with my sons.
The world is something else
when we get altitude.

Hard to see it otherwise
even when flying alone
on the pass they give me for the flight out.

We saw the dangers long ago
and found a song or a saying
to keep us free.

At the pound we say
every dog has his day.
It doesn't mean much but it gets us by.

The railroad crossing has a song <u>and</u> a saying.
You know the song
but this is the first time
the saying's found a page —
let the low side drag
we yell, looking both ways even on green.

If the sun finds an open blind
and shows us someone sleeping
we've got the right tongue to josh him with:
Frère Jacques, Frère Jacques,
dormez-vous, dormez-vous?
The best part's when we ring
all the bells on the hill.

After that there's the valley so low
you have to hang your head over
to hear the wind blow.
We get solemn on that one
but it doesn't last.

I think they already sense I'm the old cowboy
sentimental and silly to the end.
We learned a new one today
and here I'm still humming it on the solo run:
From this valley they say you are going,
I shall miss your bright eyes and your smile.

II

On the Island

1.

Things had not been right
and you thought another place
would bring you back around to your old self.
The horoscope said a journey
under the sign of Cancer.
The madman was waiting for you
at his small airstrip beside the Gulf.

2.

And now on the island you are thinking
everything will fall back in place.
The madman is spraying the frozen moving parts
of all he owns with 3-in-1 oil:
his Shakespeare reel, the clasp on his tackle box,
the Amphi-Cat that will cart you to the edge
of the island where fish are feeding.
Things ought to go smooth
he says, shards of rust melting around him
like Baked Alaska.

3.

The crabs watch you like a Greek play
they have seen repeatedly.

4.

The surf curls with the tropes of your reel,
you are bailing line, working your lures
through the waves like a hairdresser.
Everything is going smooth
until the fish begin feasting on your baits,
striking whatever hook you throw
concealed in acrylic minnow-shine or colored feathers.

You forget the trained bones
of your wrist, the follow-through, the line's fine arc.
You throw your whole arm away
like soft-drink bottles.
You come to understand men
shooting buffalo
from the windows of trains.

5.

Where you are becomes a train
the madman is conducting
and it trundles you and your gasping luggage
to night around the butane's blue eye
in his driftwood hotel.
The stubs of that trip in your hand,
soaked in Wild Turkey sours and fried fish,
you hear how the vacuum-cleaner salesman
brought his secretary to pure frenzy
with stag films on a motel wall.
The joke was the bellboy
eyeing the projector in its squat case.
Traveling light.
The haberdasher has one better than that:
the woman and the goat . . . Spanish fly in her drink . . .
Outside the crabs go wild as turkeys,
imagining the soft shells of your women
and edging toward the waste heap at the door.

6.

On the second day in the surf
the shark will take the blues away
from the stringer floating too close to your hip.
You think of your white poplin legs
strutting like a minstrel show in his aquarium,
how he can make a legless singing toy of you.

But do not fret — since he cannot dance
on your legs back into his twelve-part band
he is probably only after the one fish that knows
the celestial step, the shared part, of his sign;
your few remaining hours here belong to the fiddler,
the spider, perhaps a random limulus.
Their sign is now everywhere around you.

7.

Distress has swooped a plane over the island
to bring the cannister with muslin flagging its fall.
Inside, a message for the madman:
COME AT ONCE
THE RIVER IS ON FIRE
ALL THROUGH YOUR CITY
MEASURES ARE BEING TAKEN
His only prospect a horizon dark with carbon,
he has flown off into the sunset
like a desperate measure of his own.

8.

And now high tide makes a cut
through the thin island.
You cannot hear
what they are saying on the other side,
figures weaving in their own boozy moon,
bodies glistening with spindrift.
You hear only the collapse
of waves, the shark's parting song,
the rasp of crabs dancing on sand.
Soon they will be moving
all over your body,
burning you down
like the things of the earth
you could not live with.

III

Another Sentimental Journey

> "Time is a tease. Time is a tease —
> because everything has to happen
> in its own time." — *Nadja*

Here is something from the past this morning,
outside the raised shade,
something you suppose the wind has blown
up to the French doors of the bedroom.

It is a Time-Life disc
from an ad that came in the mail,
Sentimental Journey on one side,
blank on the other,
part of an offer that said there is more,
there is much much more.

If you could mend
where the dog's teeth broke through
before he dropped it at your door
(not the wind after all),
smooth the wrinkles,
and get just a snatch of what the past danced to,
wouldn't you order the whole package?

Isn't that enough —
a little teasing from Time?
You don't really want to reach out
in a past time, do you,
and find again that something
has come between your hand
and the flimsy curtain
you want to pull away?

The Ballet of Happiness

A letter comes from the city today
where she has just gone,
my student of a year ago,
to study art.
She says it is a long story
and asks among other things
if I am happy.

Instead of an answer of my own to send back,
I think of what she once gave
to the same question: she said no, not much,
but went on to name what in recent memory
had made her happy:

It was friends calling in the moonlight
to her balcony, saying they had come
to dance for her The Ballet of Happiness.
Which they did, their bright mescaline eyes
smiling up at her, and when it was over
they bowed like children in a play
and left — just walked across the grass,
leaving her dazzled and happy
with the funny shapes of their footwork
fading in the dew.

I have carried that dance a year in my head,
not realizing until now that for us too
friends appear on the damp lawn
and give us their blurred version
of a story they want to live
where image arises from image, freely,
and their kind bodies move for the words.

And we can be happy
because they have not come to take anything
but our smile
which we give in the freest of associations,
for they may never come again
or else forget and stay too long.

So am I happy?
It is a long story
and my feet are moving into moonlight
like clouds; friends are waiting.

The New Rheostat

for Vereen & Jane

You are proud
you put it in with your own hands
and so I ask you
to show me your favorite setting.
Allowing for candles I have to imagine,
you turn it down.
This is how it will be
some evening soon:
there are no place cards;
we are free
to move in this illumination
as if the moment were unconditional.
It is like going to bed
and finding our old bodies,
the faces we wore in the caves,
the light the water dimmed.

What Lasts
for Gerald

'They'll be memories'
he said of the pictures you'd just taken of us
and there was nothing we could add to that.
The simple man had said his simple truth.
Off Hatteras we will remember years later,
seeing the prints, *out along the Gulf Stream*
where the water is two colors.
And so we could not tell him 'nothing lasts'
or point to the dolphin
fading in the hold of our boat
or work aloud with what he had said
as though it were a passage in a text.
We could only nod and say he was right,
thinking to ourselves it was a good way
of keeping the idea simple: how these images
would develop into a history
the mind has amended to its own needs —
like your medley from the Fifties
or your story of having to kiss Big Arms
in the burnt-out casino
or stories of the trouble we've all had with *flux* —
thinking those things and smiling
as if for a moment in the play of light and water
we could believe there was no more to it than that.

The hummingbird that tried to fly through the glass of your big window last summer like a plane of light, was it bringing you a promise?

How long can you hold out in that living room?

When you found the hummingbird, weren't ants working the channels of its body like spiritual electricians wiring the wing of a cathedral for miracles?

Drilling for Fire

for my students
who have lost sleep over it

Even if it were for real
it would not be a fire worth remembering
or losing sleep over,
not in this stone block —

a mattress maybe, or plaid curtains
someone's mother sent,
but nothing to light up the sky
like a celebration,
nothing that would touch you
and leave a mark

like the girl who has come into your room
while you wait twelve floors down
for the all-clear sign.

At this precise moment
she is pulling the red sweep-second hand
off your clock,
knowing you never needed that fine a reading.

But you do not yet know of your losses;
echoes are entering your head
like sleet drilling an open pond
and someone is saying there is no fire,
no need for water,
return to your room.

You are moving back up the stairwell
to where your door offers back your name.
Inside you realize that things are missing.

Cuff links are gone,
your sleeves flap in the wind from the hall.
Your baby book, your high-school yearbook,
all your scrapbooks are open on the desk
where she has cut your pictures out
and pasted in an invitation to a party
for the misunderstood,
an obsolete flight schedule,
the label from a jar of facial cream,
an ad for a tour of the homes
of movie stars.

You try to remember your face in the pictures.
All that comes to you is the time
you used the thin sweep-second
to see how long you could hold your breath.
Not long enough to suit you.

And all the other that is missing?
On your tape recorder
she has left you clues
to where you can eventually find
the whole cache
if you want it back.
A scavenger hunt that will take
the rest of your life.

Finally she says
she thinks she ought to tell you
she is your mother,

no your sister,
no no the first girl you entered,
no she means your future wife
or your present one or one you lusted after secretly,
or rather a woman
you never knew
and she is waiting for you
in a place you might not recognize
if you decide to come, begging her
to say what else should be forgotten.

You must decide, though,
and tell yourself what kind of recovery you want:

you can go with clues
toward cuff links and buttons,
things you used to hold yourself together,
a measured breath, old preventive devices,
lapsed membership cards,
and other mementoes.

or else you can start on your own
toward her voice.

For the time being
you are in ashes everywhere you turn.
What can you say?

But wait,
the pool of blue in your bed, she says,
will furnish you with words you've denied yourself:
dip your pen there in sleep

and write your life on the wall
in the language of dreams.
The empty ink bottle on the floor —
fill it with small stones and cinders
from along the interstate
as you go on wherever you've told yourself.
Study the reductions that have taken place.
There in the bottle — study your life
as though it were on fire.

Shining Testaments

Say we didn't know
and kept eating fish
from the waters of commerce.
The mercury dances in us
like St. Vitus.
This is history.
All it offers is the felt hat
and the penny arcade.
Sit still. Say *whiskey*.
These are the four snapshots
of your bright demise.

It All Comes Together
Outside the Restroom in Hogansville

It was the hole for looking in
only I looked out
in daylight that broadened
as I brought my eye closer.
First there was a '55 Chevy
shaved and decked like old times
but waiting on high-jacker shocks.
Then a sign that said J. D. Hines Garage.
In J. D.'s door was an empty Plymouth
with the windows down and the radio on.
A black woman was singing in Detroit
in a voice that brushed against the face
like the scarf
turning up in the wrong suitcase
long ago after everything came to grief.
What was inside we can only imagine —
men I guess trying to figure what would make it
work again. Beyond them
beyond the cracked engine blocks and thrown pistons
beyond that failed restroom
etched with our acids beyond that American Oil Station
beyond the oil on the ground
the mobile homes all over Hogansville
beyond our longing
all Georgia was green.
I'd had two for the road
a cheap enough thrill
and I wanted to think
I could take only what aroused me.
The interstate to Atlanta was wide open.

I wanted a different life.
So did J. D. Hines. So did the voice on the radio.
So did the man or woman
who made the hole in the window.
The way it works is this:
we devote ourselves to an image
we can't live with and try to kill
anything that suggests it could be otherwise.

The Tree Man at the Parthenon Tourist

Probably once a month
I see his truck of trees
parked overnight at the tourist home
and I wonder what brings him there.
Most of the big truckers
keep on trucking.
I want to think it has to do
with all the elephant ears,
not the replica of the Parthenon
down the street.
I want to see him one summer evening,
the tree man, sitting out on the porch
with the proprietress, dreaming
the one rain forest in Nashville.
But that can't be the only reason.
I called the lady and she said
she has to take them in
when the first frost falls.
And in the basement they die off
for the winter.
What about those bare months, tree man?
All your greenwood trees
are for the new rich in Chattanooga or Atlanta.
Is it that she's promised to take you down
to where the whole elephant walks,
and on into that secret graveyard
all the white hunters dream of?
Or are you trying, tree man,
to remember something forever?

The Hand That Becomes You

The glove that washed up on the beach,
shake the hand out and wear it home.
It quite becomes you.
The knots you could never master—
clove hitches, carrick bends, Matthew Walkers, Blackwall
    hitches—
are now yours and instinctively
you start securing things
that might be swept over.
By nightfall you are put in mind of the breasts of port whores
rousing in your palm,
there are flashes of bayside bars, a mixture of foreign tongues.
You find yourself buying heavy wool turtlenecks in dark colors,
calling your dog *mate*.
One morning you wake hungover,
an anchor tatooed on your forearm.
The interior decorator comes and you tell him
do it all nautical. Rigging is installed.
Men begin bringing a great store of food to your cellar
and one morning you feel your hand wince at the sight of cable
coiling around the windlass.
Realizing you are weighing anchor, you tell your hand
eight bells and all is well, all is well!
You pledge your trust in it,
promising never to let it get caught short-handed again.
It comes out of your pocket gladly to cast the mooring away
and you heave forth a mighty blessing of profanities
that astound you and bring joy to the hearts of your shipmates.
They are saying there is a New World out there,
you lucky bastard you, a New World,
islands of spice and fruit and friendly natives
ever willing to give a helping hand.

The Quintessential Pencil

On theme day they give me the shaft
of diamond sheathed in living cypress
to write my theme.
I think Clarity! Brilliance! Quiddity!
But first to negotiate a point
on the blunt end:
buzz buzz and then a brilliant shriek
like nerves at the roots of my wisdom teeth.
Clearly I need a softer core, and that is what I say.
I am handed a handful of graphite dust, splints of wood.
My theme, I think, must be Splinters. Dust.
No, no, consider the chaotic diamond in your palm,
they say, the sturdy pith.
Okay, I say, thinking instead of my heavenly body.

IV

The Motion of Bodies

I.

Two bodies attracting each other
mutually describe similar figures
about their common centre of
gravity, and about each other mutu-
ally. — Newton, *The Motion of
Bodies,* Book I, Proposition 57,
Theorem 20.

As two skaters are drawn out of their strangeness
to an open space on the ice,
so our bodies are drawn to this opening.
And as easily as the skaters move into descriptions
of, say, the common figure 8,
so we discover the figures
that mutually describe our correspondence,
each curve leading into another
more outrageous than the last.
Hard to resist the notion
that these figures have infinite possibilities,
the way we defy the gravity of this place.

II.

If a rare medium consist of very
small quiescent particles of equal
magnitudes, and freely disposed at
equal distances from one another: to
find the resistance of a globe moving
uniformly forwards in this medium.
— Book II, Proposition 35,
Problem 7.

Imagine the medium
consists of the small particles of my vision.
I cannot call them rare,
but toward the fine apparatus of your breasts
as you move uniformly forwards in this medium,
they are uncommonly quiescent and freely disposed.
Move deeper into the condition
and feel these particles of my seeing surround your body,
impinging enough to prove their equal magnitudes,
yet giving way enough to suggest
that our findings are close at hand:
the perfect resistances, the solid proof.

III.

There is no oval figure whose area,
cut off by right lines at pleasure, can
be universally found by means of
equations of any number of finite
terms and dimensions. — Book I,
Lemma 28.

These are the right lines at pleasure,
no question.
I'd even try to revive a worn figure
and say we're floating
in a balloon of our own design
but that would leave out too much —
the way your body's curves
confer with space, for instance,
in terms so elliptical
they've taken on the dimensions of mystery.
The best we can do
to avoid the possible clouds of suspicion
is press on, we sense, casting the lines
and tending the small flame
that holds us aloft.

IV.

All motion propagated through a
fluid diverges from a rectilinear pro-
gress into the unmoved spaces.
— Book II, Proposition 42,
Theorem 33.

See yourself as the fluid medium
through which this motion is propagated.
We both are swimmers there,
I in you, and you in yourself with me.
Feel the progressions of our strokes
follow their given lines
until finally a motion in each of us breaks
and diverges into the unmoved spaces,
the still water that waits like a sky
for the crescents ringing our bodies.

V.

To find the distances of the pulses.
— Book II, Proposition 50,
Problem 12.

We'd have to find time and space.
As a rule, I can count on my hands
but right now they're tuned
to the quartz crystals strumming in your body,
the only timepiece they trust.
So don't move, let everything
take its own good time.

v

Natural Growth

Plant your eyes in the solid bank of trees,
in the room where the pines are counting their long green.
Let your vision grow into the other kingdom.
Look at it this way:
if cows come
grass is happy to be straw
in the mortar that holds the meadow together.
Poppies support their habits
through only the most benevolent of aggressions.
The willow on the river's eroding ledge
says *no money in the bank*
but still it joins its family in green huzzas
for light and space.
That's when you can tell
if your eyes have taken root:
every cheer that reaches you is one
you know by heart.

Family Business

Same provisions season after season,
nothing fancy. But they keep the doors open
even after the others have rolled in
their awnings and gone to the islands.
The plain sign beaming in the snow
satisfaction guaranteed
evergreen   evergreen

A Question of the Elements

'Help me keep my powder dry,'
I pled with the flood, 'I'll back your cause.'
'Can't play favorites,' it whispered,
'stand tall, you'll get the word: *river on the rise.*'

I tuned in the lightning,
asked 'what tree next?'
'Stay low,' was all it said,
'I'll give you the sign.'

I wired the wind for hints or charts;
answer came 4th-class mail:
'I play the earth's curve, lover boy,
you plot it.'

Finally there is nowhere to turn but earth,
crying 'I'm yours.'
'You can count on me,' it yawns,
'would I let you down?'

The Green World

Move through it
as though it were a house whose windows
your breath has been floating
in and out of from birth.

The attic of course is full
of the essential stuff—the wedding veil,
an old box camera, water-colors, the winning thesis.
Whatever we thought was worn out.

In the root cellar
is the food we will need for the winter.
There's wine down there too.
Drive you out of your head.

Sorry we forgot to mark the years
on the bottles. Some are better than others,
but there's no way
you can be sure.

We'll watch for you
to come reeling up the stairwell.
Just don't knock over the lantern
or wake up the children.

The best view's from the verandah.
Always a spare chair or two.
Birds chirp, dogs bark.
You can see the bend of the river.

Make yourself at home.

VI

I don't think I'll ever get over women.
— Gerald Duff

Devices

The one of lambskin
I left in Sardis Lake that night:
tell the girl whose body print surrounds it
I said
come back to the water.

Whatever came between us . . .
nothing's been settled.

I don't understand
what passes between women and me
any more than I used to.
Naked and proud, I'm still the sailor
who had his body
tattooed like an admiral's uniform.

One woman told me a little pain
never hurt anybody.
Well, it doesn't go very far either.
The sharpest tooth I ever felt
left only a bruise
easing along under the thumbnail
like an old turtle,
purple and dry
and almost a friend by the end.

So I'm saying come back to the water.
Somebody keeps calling long distance
whispering the coast is clear.
It's probably the voice-whores again
in some bar with their voyeur friends,
but I promise I'll try
to give them the slip this time
if you'll chant it again
and again *Don't tell don't tell*

One of the Big Differences

I slept with a girl steady once
who stole water glasses from the grill—
two or three a week in her purse,
each one dumb with its lip dream.
The last kiss, though, was for the brick wall
bracing itself behind the oilman's dorm.
I was dumb too in my own caul of thirst:
when the moon pulled her down one dark month
with the lost water, she broke us all
out of our vows, the identical O's,
a man's name on every one and mine the last
echoing that she bled and we couldn't care.
Cut yourself to ribbons
getting out of that girl's hair.

Dreamboat

My dreamboat comes in a dream.
She is ugly and my friends are there.
When they are gone
and I am alone with her
she is beautiful again
as in life.
Why does she do me that way?

The Body Breaking in the Glass House

Your body almost believed it was holding out
last night at dinner in the glass house.

Just beyond the fractions of light from other rooms
all outdoors was breaking into April
close enough to touch
and your body was saying it would last,
it would last.

It would last
until you raised the Chablis to your lips
and glimpsed the body
of your hostess's young daughter
reflected in the facing wall of glass
too brief to tell
whether she was simply bringing another tray
of toast sticks with caraway seeds
or had truly slipped outside her linen dress
like April, blind to the light
that gathers toward the sheer wall.

Either way, in or out of linen,
it all broke from the glass
close enough to touch
and left you trying to keep your head
from slumping backward into the crewelwork,
nodding yes yes to her father's hand of white wine
or any small thing from the tray
her mother held before you.

VII

Patching Up the Past with Water

1.

For a beginning
let yourself be drawn like debris
to all the great bodies of water;
I will be there
asking you to help
lift up a hand of water
and reach into a time
we dream to change.
No matter that even before
your first palm is taken away
the water washes off itself
like quicksilver off a wall of glass
or that your hand becomes a broken colander
wired loosely to the wrist,
sieving whatever drifts by,
no matter—we also want to keep an eye peeled
for anything that might give the past away:
bits and pieces, twigs and such.
We can begin anywhere
you find an entry.

2.

It could be a key
from the Hotel Pemaquid
where the room keys have all been lost
over the years.
For ventilation, the desk clerk will say,
just leave the door ajar
and pull the door curtain for privacy,

nothing has ever been stolen.
Find the room matching your secret key,
lock yourself in and ponder
the clutter of your uninsurable goods,
the fog that curtains
the Maine coast by morning.
Listen as confusion sweeps up the maid service
when they arrive at your door screaming
nothing has ever been stolen, there is someone
needing to trust you
in every room on the hall.
You see your door as *out there*
and fumble to unlock it
through the drape of fog.
The dead air, the foggy misapprehension, the unimaginable
water.
Anything to help you understand
this history better.

3.

A song maybe
but nothing resembling this stone shore.
Someone in lime-green half-sleeves
knows the words. South of here.
The instruments are in fake alligator cases
piled near the lake in the grass,
and he is stretching his arms
toward the one he can chord for this song,
seeing us walk the line
off the interstate.
His band, blowing smoke over the lake
and waiting for the Plymouth to cool down

to their chill lime shirts,
will hear the song come off the water,
blue grass,
and give him the rest of the music
his words need.
They forget the VFW dance three hundred miles away —
these are the old words
they can't leave alone,
broke with love again and singing.
We know now that peace won't come
the whole night through.

4.

A dream drifts by, one that recurs:
the bride your wife once was
is the one Mayans dress in precious metals
and stones for the sacrificial lake.
And now a guided tour back by steamer
to the waterfall above her pool:
you, your miserable guide,
the deserted concession stand.
But the dream changes; in this one
you are alone.
In the water the riches you have been coming for
are nothing but silt
except for eyes brighter than any fire,
reaching you like hands.
Whatever the old ritual denied
has been yours for the taking all along.

5.

If the rain comes
let it take you back.
What was it your father brought you
in his voice out of the rain?
You breathed your question alone in the rear seat
that night in the middle of the field
when he came back to the car with your youngest uncle
and the sack of frogs from another man's pond.
The brief interior light
from the opened door in his face
gave you that question and part of its answer;
his changed voice told you more:
the man whose sounds were lost in the dark rain
had caught them at his pond's edge.
That much was available at the border
of their words in the car
as they tried to talk away from you,
but you would never know the secret of their tremor.
Now in the rain
you ask your father to take you back,
show you where the man came out of the trees
down to his pond,
say what was said and done,
not to turn away.

6.

For long spells at a time
any leaf we turn over

turns out to be the chemical paper
where a Polaroid picture cleared

and was torn away.
We trace the shadows of its slate gravestone
as though we were doing a temple rubbing,
and always the ghost of a woman
emerges in silver at the water's edge.
Three frames away, a white heron
in flight, the same day, the same water.
That's when the tracings in our hands
take flight or else become a montage
of all the wrong that lovers always do.
Nothing we can do but return
to where our decoys are waiting in their dream
and there resume whittling at the worn reed of desire
that calls up time after time
from its wooden throat
enough down here for us both.

7.

Eventually this intimation:
some matters water won't solve.
Her divorce was four years ago.
Here are new friends, white wine on ice,
and the cigarette coming back around from hand to hand
on this Saturday afternoon where Leaf River eases south
out of a little town in Mississippi called Petal.
She had to get free. You can understand:
he was the one who hung the gaudy dress in her closet.
Leaf and petal, she is thinking,
wash it all away but leaf and petal.
But still his image flashes up
with its one lesson: *root and stalk.*
And water won't tell why.

8.

Children hear what water tells best of all.
It calls up to them from the river
walk out of the empty mansion on the bluff
and find the sundial in the garden.
The line looped around its pedestal
will lead you down the hill to the white boat.
Cut it loose and let it drift away.
Be free of the death they planned for you.
It wasn't malice; they painted the boat each summer
and remembered the customary favors.
Wave your love up the slope to them
and ease into the water.
Follow your death only as far as you have to.

9.

So much in our mothers' eyes
we could not help.
I think of a photograph
of my own mother at seventeen.
She is kneeling beside a lily pond
in someone's yard.
The bathing suit is a one-piece wool jersey
and her body is almost as white as the clouds.
No man has seen it all.
There are goldfish in the water
her hand is in,
but we cannot see them.

Now she has lifted her face to the camera
and I am wishing we could be true —
my father, my sisters,
you and I, all of us
waiting out here in the future
like the stone frog her other hand rests on.

10.

Somewhere your hand or mine
will come to rest
on the water table bearing only itself,
the true food of this dream.
In it we taste fossils, clouds, failure.
For all our palms of water, our sieving,
this is what we come to,
a water that offers nothing
from the private past,
water that down to its last
and smallest particle resists our will.
As it begins to move through us
we feel its secret in each lapse
of our pulse *no one moment separate from another*
no one motion
Never that dreamed absence of succession
in which to reassemble the whole being.
And yet our hands are straining
as though some image, free and alterable,
had dropped from the table
and lay within reach.